Copyright © 2025 by Educate Learners

Published by Educate Learners

All rights reserved. No part of this publication may be reproduced, distributed, or transmitted in any form or by any means, including photocopying, recording, or other electronic or mechanical methods, without the prior written permission of the publisher, except in the case of brief quotations embodied in critical reviews and certain other noncommercial uses permitted by copyright law.

First Printing, 2025.

ISBN: 978-1-951573-60-7

www.educatelearners.com

This is a doctor. A doctor keeps us healthy.

Doctors
Do annual check-ups
Treat sickness and injury
Prescribe medicine
Perform surgery

This is a veterinarian. A veterinarian helps injured and sick animals.

Veterinarians
Work with animals, only
Treat sickness and injury
Perform surgery
Give vaccinations

This is a firefighter.
A firefighter puts out fires.

Firefighters
Extinguish fires
Rescue people from fires
Rescue pets from fires
Teaches fire safety

This is a mail carrier. A mail carrier delivers mail.

Mail Carriers

Pick up mail
Deliver letters
Deliver packages
Get mail to the right address

This is a farmer.
A farmer grows
the food we eat.

Farmers

Grow fruits and veggies
Grow grains and beans
Raise animals we eat
Sell to grocery stores

This is a bus driver.
A bus driver drives our school bus.

Bus Drivers

Drive us to school
Drive us home
Drive us to field trips
Keep us safe on the bus

This is a librarian
A librarian helps us get library books

Librarians

Order books

Help you borrow books

Organize books

Give book information

This is a dentist. A dentist helps keep our teeth healthy.

Dentists
Clean teeth
Remove cavities
Treat disease and injury
Provide dental surgery

This is a nurse.
A nurse helps doctors keep us healthy.

Nurses
Give shots
Check blood pressure
Check temperature
Give medication

This is a police officer.
A police officer helps keep us safe.

Police Officers

Patrol the city

Solve crimes

Arrest criminals

Enforce laws

This is a mechanic. A mechanic fixes our cars.

Mechanics
Identify car issues
Fix cars issues
Fix flat tires
Change car oil

This is a cashier
A cashier helps us buy food and clothes

Cashiers

Get prices

Collect money

Bag food and clothing

Help answer questions

This is a teacher.
A teacher helps us learn.

Teachers
Teach academic skills
Organize classroom
Test your knowledge
Give you grades

This is a trash collector. A trash collector removes trash.

Trash Collectors

Pick up trash and waste
Take trash to landfills
Help keep cities clean
Help with sanitation

Thank you for reading!

Get a free year long subscription to our online education resource library when you purchase any one of our books.

Code: EDBOOKS

educatelearners.com